PIETER BRUEGHEL   THE OLD SHEPHERD

The Elder
PETER BRUEGEL

The Elder
PETER BRUEGEL
1528(?) - 1569

With an Essay by ALDOUS HUXLEY

And a Note by JEAN VIDEPOCHE

WILLEY BOOK CO. ⸱ PUBLISHERS

NEW YORK

1938

REPRODUCTIONS OF PAINTINGS BY
The Elder PETER BRUEGEL
THROUGH THE COURTESY OF
NEW YORK GRAPHIC SOCIETY

First Printing, January, 1938

This book on *The Elder* PETER BRUEGEL is one of a carefully planned series, about significant artists, published by WILLEY BOOK CO. Each book, in addition to authoritative text, contains well-selected examples of the artist's work, of which at least six are in full color and twenty-four in black and white.

BRUEGEL PLATES (Color)

SUMMER (COLOR)

AUTUMN (COLOR)

WINTER (COLOR)

THE OLD SHEPHERD (COLOR)

THE PEASANT DANCE (COLOR)

THE WEDDING FEAST (COLOR)

BRUEGEL PLATES (Black and White)

1. DETAIL FROM MASSACRE OF THE INNOCENTS
2. TOWER OF BABEL
3. CONVERSION OF ST. PAUL
4. DETAIL FROM CALVARY (MATER DOLOROSA)
5. DETAIL FROM THE ROAD TO CALVARY (THE CONDEMNED)
6. DETAIL FROM CARNIVAL AND LENT
7. DETAIL FROM PEASANT DANCE (KERMESS)—MUSICIANS
8. FEAST OF ST. MARTIN
9. PROVERB OF THE BIRD—NESTER
10. THE BATTLE OF CARNIVAL AND LENT
11. MASSACRE OF THE INNOCENTS
12. DETAIL FROM WEDDING FEAST (THE MUSICIANS)
13. DETAIL FROM WEDDING FEAST (EATING PIE)
14. CHILDREN'S GAMES
15. DETAIL FROM WINTER
16. DETAIL FROM WEDDING FEAST (PEASANTS)
17. DETAIL FROM WINTER—THE FIRE
18. DETAIL FROM CARNIVAL AND LENT (CHURCH)
19. MARINE
20. BATTLE OF MT. GILBOA
21. THE ROAD TO CALVARY
22. DETAIL FROM THE PEASANT WEDDING
23. DETAIL FROM CHILDREN'S GAMES
24. THE ADORATION OF THE MAGI

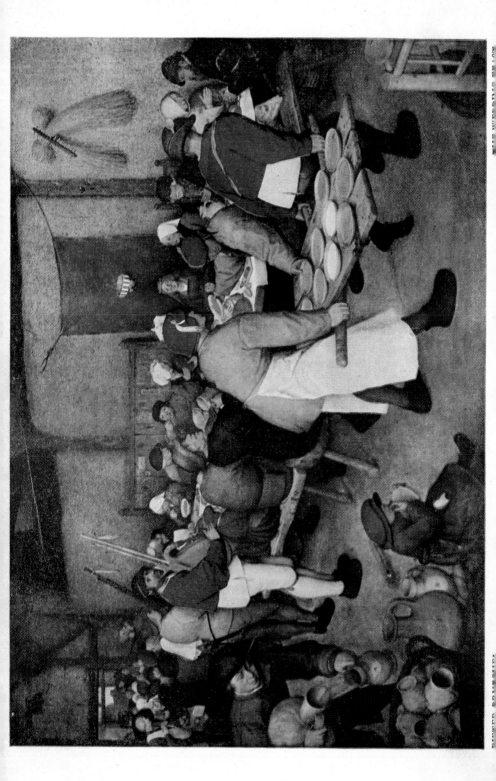

The Elder PETER BRUEGEL

1528 (?) - 1569

MOST OF OUR mistakes are fundamentally grammatical. We create our own difficulties by employing an inadequate language to describe facts. Thus, to take one example, we are constantly giving the same name to more than one thing, and more than one name to the same thing. The results, when we come to argue, are deplorable. For we are using a language which does not adequately describe the things about which we are arguing.

The word "painter" is one of those names whose indiscriminate application has led to the worst results. All those who, for whatever reason and with whatever intentions, put brushes to canvas and make pictures, are called without distinction, painters. Deceived by the uniqueness of the name, aestheticians have tried to make us believe that there is a single painter-psychology, a single function of painting, a single standard of criticism. Fashion changes and the views of art critics with it. At the present time it is fashionable to believe in form to the exclusion of subject. Young people almost swoon away with excess of aesthetic emotion before a Matisse. Two generations ago they would have been wiping their eyes before the latest Landseer. (Ah, those more than human, those positively Christ-like dogs—how they moved, what lessons they taught! There had been no religious painting like Landseer's since Carlo Dolci died.)

These historical considerations should make us chary of be-
lieving too exclusively in any single theory of art. One kind of
painting, one set of ideas are fashionable at any given moment.
They are made the basis of a theory which condemns all other
kinds of painting and all preceding critical theories. The process
constantly repeats itself.

At the present moment, it is true, we have achieved an unpre-
cedentedly tolerant eclecticism. We are able, if we are up-to-date,
to enjoy everything, from negro sculpture to Luca della Robbia
and from Magnasco to Byzantine mosaics. But it is an eclecticism
achieved at the expense of almost the whole content of the
various works of art considered. What we have learned to see in
all these works is their formal qualities, which we abstract and
arbitrarily call essential. The subject of the work, with all that
the painter desired to express in it beyond his feelings about formal relations, contemporary criticism rejects as unimportant. The
young painter scrupulously avoids introducing into his pictures
anything that might be mistaken for a story, or the expression of
a view of life, while the young *Kunstforscher* turns, as though at
an act of exhibitionism, from any manifestation by a contemporary of any such forbidden interest in drama or philosophy.
True, the old masters are indulgently permitted to illustrate
stories and express their thoughts about the world. Poor devils,
they knew no better! Your modern observer makes allowance
for their ignorance and passes over in silence all that is not a
matter of formal relations. The admirers of Giotto (as numerous
to-day as were the admirers of Guido Reni a hundred years ago)
contrive to look at the master's frescoes without considering what
they represent, or what the painter desired to express. Every germ

of drama or meaning is disinfected out of them; only the composition is admired. The process is analogous to reading Latin verses without understanding them—simply for the sake of the rhythmical rumbling of the hexameters.

It would be absurd, of course, to deny the importance of formal relations. No picture can hold together without composition and no good painter is without some specific passion for form as such—just as no good writer is without a passion for words and the arrangement of words. It is obvious that no man can adequately express himself, unless he takes an interest in the terms which he proposes to use as his medium of expression. Not all painters are interested in the same sort of forms. Some, for example, have a passion for masses and the surfaces of solids. Others delight in lines. Some compose in three dimensions. Others like to make silhouettes on the flat. Some like to make the surface of the paint smooth and, as it were, translucent, so that the objects represented in the picture can be seen distinct and separate, as through a sheet of glass. Others (as for example Rembrandt) love to make a rich thick surface which shall absorb and draw together into one whole all the objects represented, and that in spite of the depth of the composition and the distance of the objects from the plane of the picture. All these purely aesthetic considerations are, as I have said, important. All artists are interested in them; but almost none are interested in them to the exclusion of everything else. It is very seldom indeed that we find a painter who can be inspired merely by his interest in form and texture to paint a picture. Good painters of "abstract" subjects or even of still lives are rare. Apples and solid geometry do not stimulate a man to express his feelings about form and make a composition. All thoughts and emotions are interdependent. In the words of the dear old song,

The roses round the door
Make me love mother more.

One feeling is excited by another. Our faculties work best in a congenial emotional atmosphere. For example, Mantegna's faculty for making noble arrangements of forms was stimulated by his feelings about heroic and god-like humanity. Expressing those feelings, which he found exciting, he also expressed—and in the most perfect manner of which he was capable—his feelings about masses, surfaces, solids and voids. "The roses round the door"—his hero worship—"made him love mother more"—made him, by stimulating his faculty for composition, paint better. If Isabella d'Este had made him paint apples, table napkins and bottles, he would have produced, being uninterested in these objects, a poor composition. And yet, from a purely formal point of view, apples, bottles and napkins are quite as interesting as human bodies and faces. But Mantegna—and with him the majority of painters—did not happen to be very passionately interested in these inanimate objects. When one is bored one becomes boring.

The apples round the door
Make me a frightful bore.

Inevitably, unless I happen to be so exclusively interested in form that I can paint anything that has a shape; or unless I hap-

1. DETAIL FROM MASSACRE OF THE INNOCENTS

2. TOWER OF BABEL

3. CONVERSION OF ST. PAUL

4. DETAIL FROM CALVARY (WATER BOLOGNA)

5. DETAIL FROM THE CALVARY (THE CONDEMNED)

6. DETAIL FROM CARNIVAL AND LENT

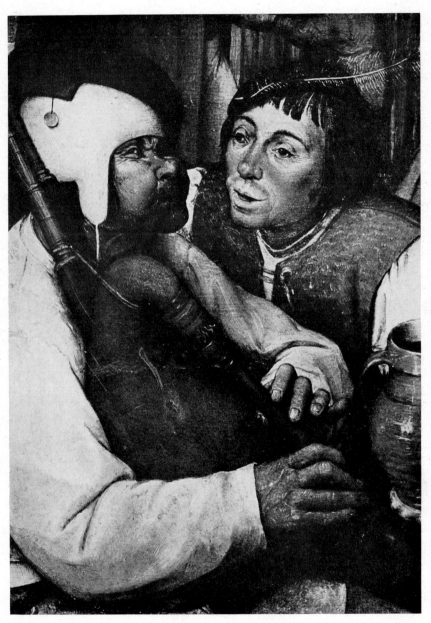

7. DETAIL FROM PEASANT DANCE (KERMESS)—MUSICIANS

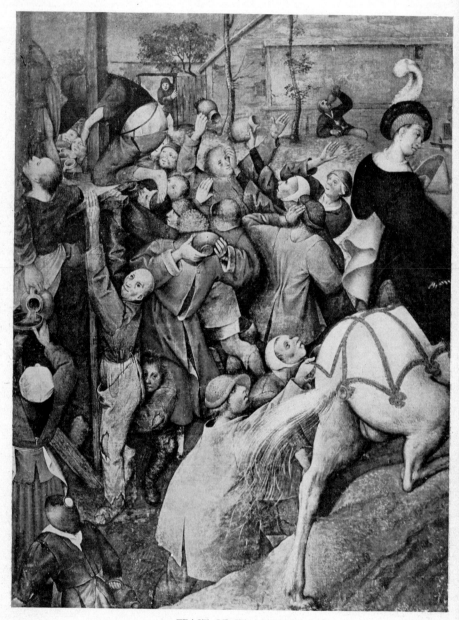

8. FEAST OF ST. MARTIN

pen to possess some measure of that queer pantheism, that animistic superstition which made van Gogh regard the humblest of common objects as being divinely or devilishly alive. *"Crains dans le mur aveugle un regard qui t'épie."* If a painter can do that, he will be able, like van Gogh, to make pictures of cabbage fields and the bedrooms of cheap hotels that shall be as wildly dramatic as a Rape of the Sabines.

The contemporary fashion is to admire beyond all others the painter who can concentrate on the formal side of his art and produce pictures which are entirely devoid of literature. Old Renoir's apophthegm, *"Un peintre, voyez-vous, qui a le sentiment du téton et des fesses, est un homme suavé,"* is considered by the purists suspiciously latitudinarian. A painter who has the sentiment of the pap and the buttocks is a painter who portrays real models with gusto. Your pure aesthete should only have a feeling for hemispheres, curved lines and surfaces. But this "sentiment of the buttocks" is common to all good painters. It is the lowest common measure of the whole profession. It is possible, like Mantegna, to have a passionate feeling for all that is solid, and at the same time to be a stoic philosopher and a hero-worshipper; possible, with Michelangelo, to have a complete realization of breasts and also an interest in the soul or, like Rubens, to have a sentiment for human greatness as well as for human rumps. The greater includes the less; great dramatic or reflective painters know everything that the aestheticians who paint geometrical pictures, apples or buttocks know, and a great deal more besides. What they have to say about formal relations, though important, is only a part of what they have to express. The contemporary insistence on form to the exclusion of everything else is an ab-

13

surdity. So was the older insistence on exact imitation and sentiment to the exclusion of form. There need be no exclusions. In spite of the single name, there are many different kinds of painters, and all of them, with the exception of those who cannot paint, and those whose minds are trivial, vulgar and tedious, have a right to exist.

All classifications and theories are made after the event; the facts must first occur before they can be tabulated and methodized. Reversing the historical process, we attack the facts forearmed with theoretical prejudice. Instead of considering each fact on its own merits, we ask how it fits into the theoretical scheme. At any given moment a number of meritorious facts fail to fit into the fashionable theory and have to be ignored. Thus El Greco's art failed to conform with the ideal of good painting held by Philip the Second and his contemporaries. The Sienese primitives seemed to the seventeenth and eighteenth centuries incompetent barbarians. Under the influence of Ruskin, the later nineteenth century contrived to dislike almost all architecture that was not Gothic. And the early twentieth century, under the influence of the French, deplores and ignores, in painting, all that is literary, reflective or dramatic.

In every age theory has caused men to like much that was bad and reject much that was good. The only prejudice that the ideal art critic should have is against the incompetent, the mentally dishonest and the futile. The number of ways in which good pictures can be painted is quite incalculable, depending only on the variability of the human mind. Every good painter invents a new way of painting. Is this man a competent painter? Has he something to say, is he genuine? These are the questions a critic must ask himself. Not, does he conform with my theory of imitation, or distortion, or moral purity, or significant form?

There is one painter against whom, it seems to me, theoretical prejudice has always most unfairly told. I mean the elder Breughel. Looking at his best paintings I find that I can honestly answer in the affirmative all the questions which a critic may legitimately put himself. He is highly competent aesthetically; he has plenty to say; his mind is curious, interesting and powerful; and he has no false pretensions, is entirely honest. And yet he has never enjoyed the high reputation to which his merits entitle him. This is due, I think, to the fact that his work has never quite squared with any of the various critical theories which since his days have had a vogue in the aesthetic world.

A subtle colourist, a sure and powerful draughtsman, and possessing powers of composition that enable him to marshal the innumerable figures with which his pictures are filled into pleasingly decorative groups (built up, as we see, when we try to analyze his methods of formal arrangement, out of individually flat, silhouette-like shapes standing in a succession of receding planes), Breughel can boast of purely aesthetic merits that ought to endear him even to the strictest sect of the Pharisees. Coated with this pure aesthetic jam, the bitter pill of his literature might easily, one would suppose, be swallowed. If Giotto's dalliance with sacred history be forgiven him, why may not Breughel be excused for being an anthropologist and a social philosopher? To which I tentatively answer: Giotto is forgiven, because we have so utterly ceased to believe in Catholic Christianity that we can easily ignore the subject matter of his pictures and concentrate only on their formal qualities; Breughel, on the other hand, is

15

unforgivable because he made comments on humanity that are still interesting to us. From his subject matter we cannot escape; it touches us too closely to be ignored. That is why Breughel is despised by all up-to-date *Kunstforschers*.

And even in the past, when there was no theoretical objection to the mingling of literature and painting, Breughel failed, for another reason, to get his due. He was considered low, gross, a mere comedian, and as such unworthy of serious consideration. Thus, the *Encyclopaedia Britannica,* which in these matters may be safely relied on to give the current opinion of a couple of generations ago, informs us, in the eleven lines which it parsimoniously devotes to Peter Breughel, that "the subjects of his pictures are chiefly humorous figures, like those of D. Teniers; and if he wants the delicate touch and silvery clearness of that master, he has abundant spirit and comic power."

Whoever wrote these words—and they might have been written by any one desirious, fifty years ago, of playing for safety and saying the right thing—can never have taken the trouble to look at any of the pictures painted by Breughel when he was a grown and accomplished artist.

In his youth, it is true, he did a great deal of hack work for a dealer who specialized in caricatures and devils in the manner of Hieronymus Bosch. But his later pictures, painted when he had really mastered the secrets of his art, are not comic at all. They are studies of peasant life, they are allegories, they are religious pictures of the most strangely reflective cast, they are exquisitely poetical landscapes. Breughel died at the height of his powers. But there is enough of his mature work in existence— at Antwerp, at Brussels, at Naples, and above all at Vienna—to expose the fatuity of the classical verdict and exhibit him for what he was: the first landscape painter of his century, the acutest student of manners, and the wonderfully skilful pictorial expounder or suggester of a view of life. It is at Vienna, indeed, that Breughel's art can best be studied in all its aspects. For Vienna possesses practically all his best pictures of whatever kind. The scattered pictures at Antwerp, Brussels, Paris, Naples and elsewhere give one but the faintest notion of Breughel's powers. In the Vienna galleries are collected more than a dozen of his pictures, all belonging to his last and best period. The Tower of Babel, the great Calvary, the Numbering of the People at Bethlehem, the two Winter Landscapes and the Autumn Landscape, the Conversion of Saint Paul, the Battle between the Israelites and the Philistines, the Marriage Feast and the Peasant's Dance—all these admirable works are here. It is on these that he must be judged.

There are four landcapes at Vienna: the Dark Day (January) and Huntsmen in the Snow (February), a November landscape (the Return of the Cattle) and the Numbering of the People at Bethlehem, which in spite of its name is little more than a landscape with figures. This last, like the February Landscape and the Massacre of the Innocents at Brussels, is a study of snow. Snow scenes lent themselves particularly well to Breughel's style of painting. For a snowy background has the effect of making all dark or coloured objects seen against it appear in the form of very distinct, sharp-edged silhouettes. Breughel does in all his compositions what the snow does in nature. All the objects in his pictures (which are composed in a manner that reminds one very much of the Japanese) are paper-thin silhouettes arranged, plane after plane, like the theatrical scenery in the depth of the stage. Consequently in the painting of snow scenes, where nature starts by imitating his habitual method, he achieves an almost disquieting degree of fundamental realism. Those hunters stepping down over the brow of the hill towards the snowy valley with its frozen ponds are Jack Frost himself and his crew. The crowds who move about the white streets of Bethlehem have their being in an absolute winter, and those ferocious troopers looting and innocent-hunting in the midst of a Christmas card landscape are a part of the very army of winter, and the innocents they kill are the young green shoots of the earth.

Breughel's method is less fundamentally compatible with the snowless landscapes of January and November. The different planes stand apart a little too flatly and distinctly. It needs a softer, bloomier kind of painting to recapture the intimate quality of such scenes as those he portrays in these two pictures. A born painter of Autumn, for example, would have fused the beasts, the men, the trees and the distant mountains into a hazier unity, melting all together, the near and the far, in the rich surface of his paint. Breughel painted too transparently and too flatly to be the perfect interpreter of such landscapes. Still, even in terms of his not entirely suitable convention he has done marvels. The Autumn Day is a thing of the most exquisite beauty. Here, as in the more somberly dramatic January Landscape, he makes a subtle use of golds and yellows and browns, creating a sober yet luminous harmony of colours. The November Landscape is entirely placid and serene; but in the Dark Day he has staged one of those natural dramas of the sky and earth—a conflict between light and darkness. Light breaks from under clouds along

18

the horizon, shines up from the river in the valley that lies in the middle distance, glitters on the peaks of the mountains. The foreground, which represents the crest of a wooded hill, is dark; and the leafless trees growing on the slopes are black against the sky. These two pictures are the most beautiful sixteenth-century landscapes of which I have any knowledge. They are intensely poetical, yet sober and not excessively picturesque or romantic. Those fearful crags and beetling precipices of which the older painters were so fond do not appear in these examples of Breughel's maturest work.

Breughel's anthropology is as delightful as his nature poetry. He knew his Flemings, knew them intimately, both in their prosperity and during the miserable years of strife, of rebellion, of persecution, of war and consequent poverty which followed the advent of the Reformation in Flanders.

A Fleming himself, and so profoundly and ineradicably a Fleming that he was able to go to Italy, and, like his great countryman in the previous century, Roger can der Weyden, return without the faintest tincture of Italianism—he was perfectly qualified to be the natural historian of the Flemish folk. He exhibits them mostly in those moments of orgiastic gaiety with which they temper the laborious monotony of their daily lives: eating enormously, drinking, uncouthly dancing, indulging in that peculiarly Flemish scatological waggery. The Wedding Feasts and the Peasants' Dance, both at Vienna, are superb examples of this anthropological type of painting. Nor must we forget those two curious pictures, the Battle between Carnival and Lent and the Children's Games. They too show us certain aspects of the joyous side of Flemish life. But the view is not of an individual scene, casually

19

seized at its height and reproduced. These two pictures are systematic and encyclopaedic. In one he illustrates all children's games; in the other all the amusements of carnival, with all the forces arrayed on the side of asceticism. In the same way he represents, in his extraordinary Tower of Babel, all the processes of building. These pictures are handbooks of their respective subjects.

Breughel's fondness for generalizing and systematizing is further illustrated in his allegorical pieces. The Triumph of Death, at the Prado, is appalling in its elaboration and completeness. The fantistic "Dulle Griet" at Antwerp is an almost equally elaborate triumph of evil. His illustrations to proverbs and parables belong to the same class. They show him to have been a man profoundly convinced of the reality of evil and of the horrors which this mortal life, not to mention eternity, hold in store for suffering humanity. The world is a horrible place; but in spite of this, or precisely because of this, men and women eat, drink and dance, Carnival tilts against Lent and triumphs, if only for a moment; children play in the streets, people get married in the midst of gross rejoicings.

But of all Breughel's pictures the one most richly suggestive of reflection is not specifically allegorical or systematic. Christ carrying the Cross is one of his largest canvases, thronged with small figures rhythmically grouped against a wide and romantic background. The composition is simple, pleasing in itself, and seems to spring out of the subject instead of being imposed on it. So much for pure aesthetics.

Of the Crucifixion and the Carrying of the Cross there are hundreds of representations by the most admirable and diverse masters. But of all that I have ever seen this Calvary of Breughel's is the most suggestive and, dramatically, the most appealing. For all other masters have painted these dreadful scenes from within, so to speak, outwards. For them Christ is the centre, the divine hero of the tragedy; this is the fact from which they start; it affects and transforms all the other facts, justifying, in a sense, the horror of the drama and ranging all that surrounds the central figure in an ordered hierarchy of good and evil. Breughel, on the other hand, starts from the outside and works inwards. He represents the scene as it would have appeared to any casual spectator on the road to Golgotha on a certain spring morning in the year A. D. 33. Other artists have pretended to be angels, painting the scene with a knowledge of its significance. But Breughel resolutely remains a human onlooker. What he shows is a crowd of people walking briskly in holiday joyfulness up the slopes of a hill. On the top of the hill, which is seen in the middle distance on the right, are two crosses with thieves fastened to them, and between them a little hole in the ground in which another cross is soon to be planted. Round the crosses, on the bare hill-top stands a ring of people, who have come out with their picnic baskets to look on at the free entertainment offered by the ministers of justice. Those who have already taken their stand round the crosses are prudent ones; in these days we should see them with camp-stools and thermos flasks, six hours ahead of time, in the vanguard of the queue for a Melba night at Covent Garden. The less provident or more adventurous people are in the crowd coming up the hill with the third and greatest of the criminals whose cross is to take the place of honour between the other two. In their anxiety not to miss any of the fun on the way up, they forget that

21

they will have to take back seats at the actual place of execution. But it may be, of course, that they have reserved their places, up there. At Tyburn one could get an excellent seat in a private box for half a crown; with the ticket in one's pocket, one could follow the cart all the way from the prison, arrive with the criminal and yet have a perfect view of the performance. In these later days, when cranky humanitarianism has so far triumphed that hangings take place in private and Mrs. Thompson's screams are not even allowed to be recorded on the radio, we have to be content with reading about executions, not with seeing them. The impresarios who sold seats at Tyburn have been replaced by titled newspaper proprietors who sell juicy descriptions of Tyburn to a prodigiously much larger public. If people were still hanged at Marble Arch, Lord Riddell would be much less rich.

That eager, tremulous, lascivious interest in blood and beastliness which in these more civilized days we can only satisfy at one remove from reality in the pages of our newspapers, was franklier indulged in Breughel's day; the naive ingenuous brute in man was less sophisticated, was given longer rope, and joyously barks and wags its tail round the appointed victim. Seen thus, impassively, from the outside, the tragedy does not purge or uplift; it appals and makes desperate; or it may even inspire a kind of gruesome mirth. The same situation may often be either tragic or comic, according as it is seen through the eyes of those who suffer or those who look on. (Shift the point of vision a little and Macbeth could be paraphrased as a roaring farce.) Breughel makes a concession to the high tragic convention by placing in the foreground of his picture a little group made up of the holy women weeping and wringing their hands. They stand quite

22

apart from the other figures in the picture and are fundamentally out of harmony with them, being painted in the style of Roger van der Weyden. A little oasis of passionate spirituality, an island of consciousness and comprehension in the midst of the pervading stupidity and brutishness. Why Breughel put them into his picture is difficult to guess; perhaps for the benefit of the conventionally religious, perhaps out of respect for tradition; or perhaps he found his own creation too depressing and added this noble irrelevance to reassure himself.

A NOTE ON PETER BRUEGEL

1528(?)-1569

by

JEAN VIDEPOCHE

IT IS CUSTOMARY, in discussing a painter long dead, to assemble a few historical facts about his period, to show, even though superficially, how his art was shaped by his times. This is not an easy matter, but with a copy of Ploetz's *Manual of Universal History* at hand, there is no reason for us to breach the convention. We can give you some notion of what was going on when Peter Bruegel was born . . . between 1520 and 1530 A. D.

Flanders, the painter's country, was part of the Netherlands, a group of 17 provinces occupying the flat lowlands along the North Sea: the Holland, Belgium, and Northern France of today. At first these provinces had been feudal states but gradually, in the course of the 13th and 14th Centuries, the important towns had become so wealthy from the manufacture of wool that they were able to buy charters for themselves. There arose a number of municipalities, practically self-governing republics, who were semi-independent vassals of feudal overlords. In many cases, the early oligarchic systems of municipal government had given way to more democratic institutions. In Bruges, for example, apprentices over 16 were allowed to vote, and in Ghent, Antwerp, Brussels, and Liege analagous situations prevailed. In the 15th

Century, despite the gradual acquisition of the Netherlands by
the House of Burgundy, the towns maintained many of their
privileges. Prosperity increased; the country became the richest
in Europe; the arts flourished. When Charles V, hereditary duke
of Burgundy, became Holy Roman Emperor and King of Spain,
the City-States wrung further concessions from him in exchange
for the money and soldiers he needed to carry on his expensive
wars.

The effect that this period, the beginning of the rise of the
bourgeoisie, is to have on the art of Bruegel, is one that a short
note like this can only adumbrate. The collapse of feudalism, the
Reformation, are aspects of what Strachey calls the struggle for
the market, of which the evolution of Flemish art towards realism
is another phase.

This evolution towards nature and reality had been begun by
the Van Eycks and is the fundamental characteristic of early
Flemish painting. Pious subjects were gradually replaced by pro-
fane ones, religious symbolism was substituted for by didacticism.
At the beginning of the 16th Century, however, there was a reaction against this tendency to free art from the rigid limits that
the church had imposed upon it. A vogue for Italian painting
swept the country. The importance of Antwerp as a commercial
city, the daily visits of Italian ships to the seaport, had doubtless
permitted the wealthy merchants and the painters they patron-
ized to see authentic examples of the Peninsula schools. The
fashion became dominant when certain of the Flemish painters
journeyed to Rome and brought back with them the influences
with which they replaced their own vigorous and independent
traditions. For unlike the Italians, the early Flemish painters

were not interested in the beauty of line that might lie beneath the heavy outer garments of the North. The crowded indoors, where the rigours of the climate so often forced them, stimulated observation of character, notation of specific detail rather than the generalizations of the grand style, produced genre subjects rather than the over-refined religious or historical ones of the Italian schools. This imitation of Italian art, promoted by Jean Gossart, Bernard van Orley, Frans Floris, Michael Cocie, etc., was obstinately resisted, first by Jerome Bosch (of whom more later), and some fifty years afterwards, Peter Bruegel.

The painter, Peter Bruegel, is the virile harvester of early Flemish realism, enriched by his own plebian love for the soil, freed from the slavish Italianism of his contemporaries. There is some tendency to regard him as a revolutionary pioneer, in respect to his subject matter, and it is probably a good idea to correct this notion at once.

As a painter of rustic manners, he was not the first. The engravers of the 15th Century had established this direction with traditional groups like *The Peasant and his Family* and the *Road to the Market*. Peasant *Dancers* had been engraved by Schongauer, Dürer and Lucas van Leyden. The panoramic kermess of H. S. Beham contained the dances, battles, weddings, processions, and other incidents that Bruegel was to depict 20 years later. Many other painters of the 16th Century explored the possibilities of subjects of this genre. The taverns and kitchens of Pierre Aertsens, certain works of Martin van Cleef are examples.

Bruegel's innovations have not to do with subject matter but with style. He was the first to view profoundly, realistically, what others had idealized or caricatured. It was his role to leave the path of Italianism taken by his contemporaries, to rediscover the direction established by the great Flemish realists, to allow no cleverness or sacrifice to nature to interfere with his simple, personal observation.

*   *   *

"Peter Bruegel was born in the neighborhood of Breda at the village from which he took his name."

Bruegel scholarship is indebted to Carel van Mander for the above quotation, and for whatever else it knows of the artist's life as well. While speaking of scholarship, it seems fitting to observe that if those who have written about Bruegel owe their biographical data to van Mander's brief notes in the *Book of Painters,* they derive most of their other substance from Rene van Bastelaer's *Pierre Brugel, L'Ancien, son oeuvre et son temps.* It is amusing to note the extent to which they borrowed from this last work, published in Brussels in 1907, without shame or acknowledgment. The present author, however, cheerfully admits his indetedness to van Bastelaer, one which all who have read the book will quickly and perhaps cynically recognize. At any rate, having indicated our sources, we can proceed once more to the borning of Bruegel with a clear conscience.

Bruegel's birth place, as van Mander describes it, is confirmed by the registers of the Guild of St. Luke of Antwerp. When he was admitted as free master in the year 1551, his name was noted as Peeter Brueghels, or Peter from the village of Brueghel. As it happens, there is no town of Brueghel near Breda. The scholars have seized upon this point with rejoicing and several monographs owe their publication to it. Of the three towns of Brue-ghel, the one near Bois-le-Duc is at present favored. Jerome Bosch came from there and his influence on Bruegel might be explained as the first one the painter had encountered.

In making Bruegel the son of a peasant, van Mander accounted for the absence of a true family name and the reason why the artist adopted that of his native village. It is evident, of course, that family names did not exist among the common people in the 16th Century. The father's served instead, as John, son of Jacob, and when a man was away from home, he would be called by the name of his village or town. This is all simple enough and not, as Paul Colin has pointed out, particularly important. But the scholars have not been satisfied with van Mander's explanation and have offered many quarrelsome theories to take its place. Among them is Lecomte's, who believed that members of the artist's family were princes, and Alphonse Wauters, who worked out a relationship with other Bruegels who were lawyers and mer-chants. Since there is nothing, apparently, to confirm these elaborately constructed hypotheses, we will content ourselves with van Mander's data until such a time as new information, if any, appears.

For people with a borrowed name, the Bruegels certainly spelled it in enough different ways. You have probably noticed and been annoyed by this already. For a long time it has been the fashion to write it as Bruegel's descendants did: BREUGHEL, and as Mr. Huxley does. This accounts, at any rate, for the pre-vailing and inaccurate pronunciation of the name as though it were German, with the dipthong sounded as "oy". In connec-tion with the "eugh" version, it is certain that the original Peter

PIETER BRUEGHEL —WINTER

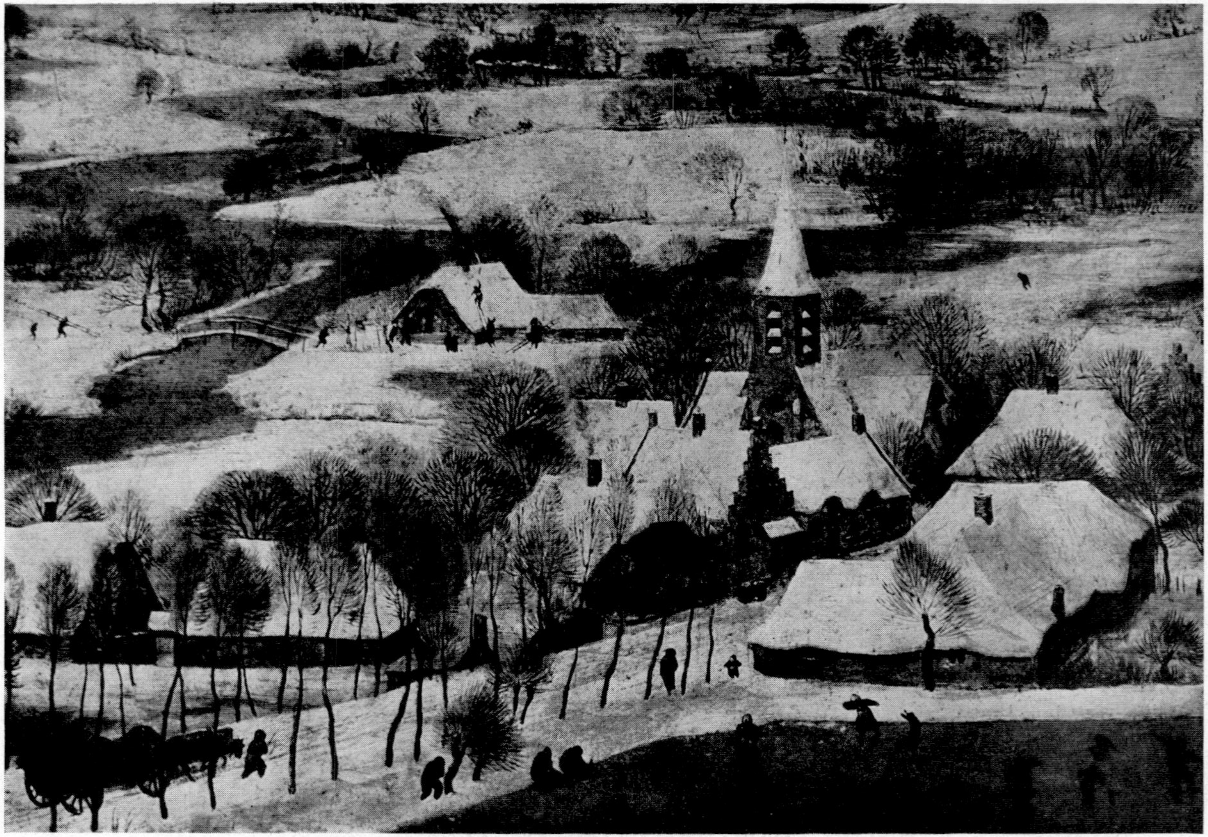

15. DETAIL FROM WINTER

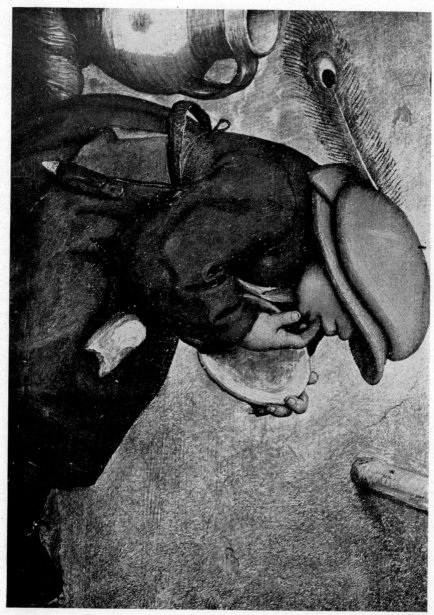

13. DETAIL FROM WEDDING FEAST (EATING PIE)

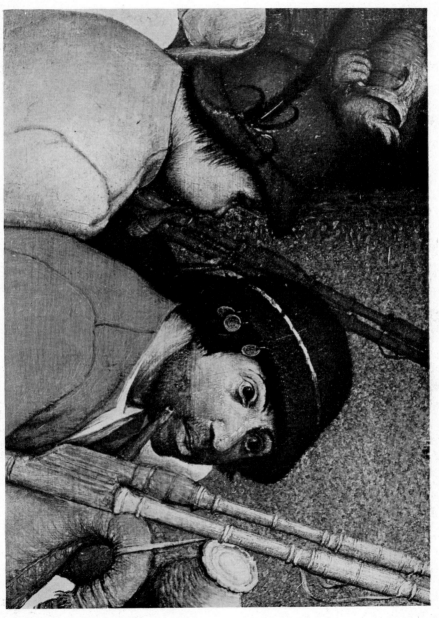

11. MASSACRE OF THE INNOCENTS

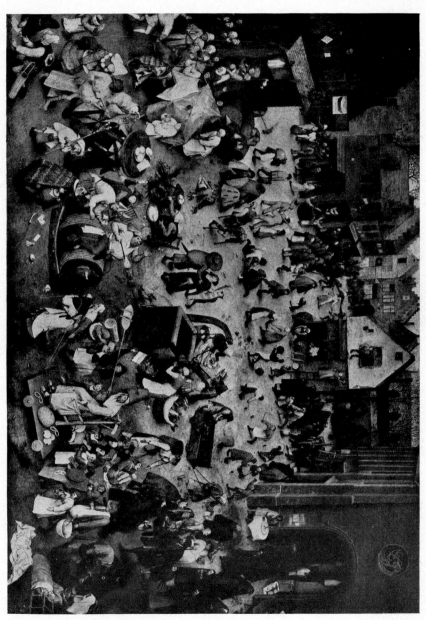

10. THE BATTLE OF CARNIVAL AND LENT

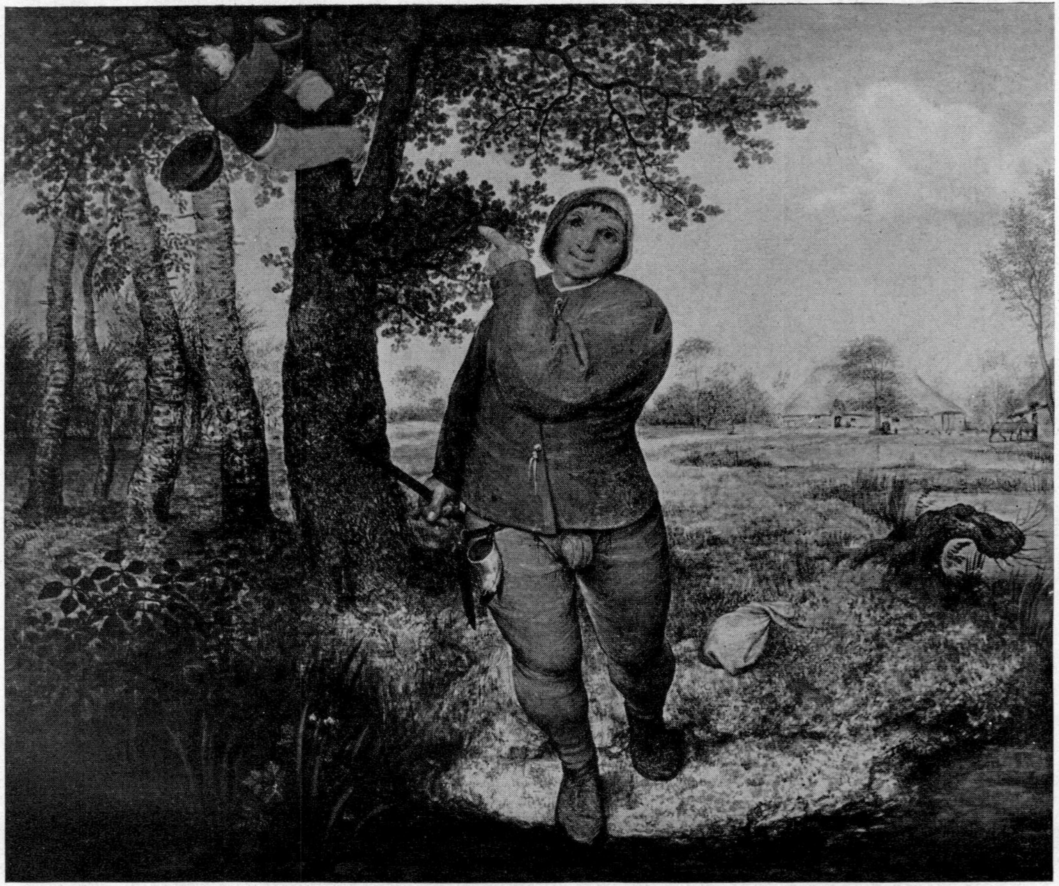

9. THE BIRD THIEF

never spelled it that way himself. All his signatures have the *e* after the *u*, as Brueghel or Bruegel.

Paul Colin has described these concerns as nonsense. This happens to be one instance among many, however, when the de-bunking point of view exceeds itself. For the business of Peter Bruegel's using the *h* in his own individualized spelling and then dropping it at a certain landmark in his development, has its very definite use. From 1551 to 1559, the period of the drawings and engravings, the painter wrote his name: *Brueghel*. In 1559, the orthography Bruegel appears at the same time as his first paintings. It is likewise signed to the engravings that appeared post 1559, the original etching and the woodcut: *Ourson et Valentin*. From 1559 to his death, the ten most important years of Bruegel's life, he is faithful to the new signature. No matter what its causes, this eccentricity helps to date the painter's work. In view of the recent attempts by certain critics like Karoly Tolnai to rearrange the Bruegel chronology so it can be made to demonstrate the theory that he was a platonist, its importance can be underestimated.

You are probably waiting impatiently, at this juncture, for some statement as to exactly when Peter Bruegel was born, and scored a mark against the author of this note for a windiness that has postponed it so long. You may have gathered, however, that the dates of both the painter's birth and his apprenticeship are unknown. Van Bastelaer has figured them approximately, using Bruegel's inscription as a free-master as a basis for his calculations. It seems a good deal easier to follow this critic's arithmetic than invent another hypothesis.

"Peeter Brueghels, schilder," was registered by the painter's guild of Antwerp in 1551. Since the average apprenticeship of a Flemish painter was six years, 1545 is indicated as the date of his entry into his profession, and sometime between 1528 to 30 as his birthdate. Van Bastelaer arrives at these conclusions by such a circuitous route that it is rather amazing, after looking back on so many pages of printed matter, to discover that the two sentences above are the result.

On Bruegel's apprenticeship, there is no data but van Mander's, and no particular reason we can see for questioning it. This chronicler says of the painter: "He was first the pupil of Peter Coeck, whose daughter he carried in his arms as a baby and later married; he passed thereafter to the discipleship of Jerome Cock and then went to France and Italy." Van Mander's casualness is to be regretted, perhaps, but it is not the result of a lack of appreciation for Bruegel whom he admired greatly. He was a contemporary of Peter's sons, and published his book around 1600, 30 years after the artist's death. Since the young Bruegels were only five years and one year old respectively when their father died, and 14 and 10 when their mother passed away, it is not surprising that they could supply little information on a parent they probably never remembered.

One can only conjecture in the absence of all information, how Peter Bruegel, a young Flemish peasant, conceived the ambition to become a painter. We shall apparently never know who encouraged him, or at what time and as a result of what circumstances he decided to go to Antwerp and apprentice himself to Peter Coeck. Van Bastelaer hazards the guess that if he were born at the Breughel near Bois-le-Duc, Bosch's town, he may have been fired by this master's example and even studied under one of his successors before going to Antwerp. Such a preliminary apprenticeship would explain both the omission of mention of his master in the register of St. Luke's Guild, since his apprenticeship was not completed in Antwerp, and the small influence upon Bruegel of a painter so influenced by the Italian Renaissance as the Coeck whom van Mander designates.

This, however, is only conjecture, and a word or two on Peter Coeck, generally accepted as Bruegel's first master, is in order. He was, according to one critic, van Orley's best pupil, according to another, his worst. A condisciple of Michael Coxcie, the "Flemish Raphael," he had made the conventional pilgrimage to Italy. There he added to the background the Italianized van Orley had given him and returned to Antwerp to practice the doctrines he absorbed for the wealthy and eager burghers. Architect, sculptor, designer of tapestry and stained glass windows, expert in the handling of both oils and water color, the versatile Peter Coeck had a brilliant and successful career. To raise the question of Coeck's influence on Bruegel may seem stupid, in view of the classic tendencies of the master and the completely opposed personality of his pupil. One could immediately affirm, and you may be sure this has been done, that Coeck's influence on Bruegel was nil. However, enamoured as Coeck was of the Italian style, he had much to teach his pupil and doubtless did exactly that. Much as it is the rule to condemn the Italian influence on Flemish painting, it would certainly, in this instance, have resulted in Bruegel's getting an excellent training in the principles of design, composition, and perspective. Further, Peter Coeck had not abandoned, like Coxcie, all his Flemish qualities. In his choice of subject matter, he appears as a painter of *mores* and reveals himself as a shrewd observer of characteristic detail. It could even be said . . . as a matter of fact it had been said . . . that Coeck influenced Bruegel and his other pupil, Nicholas Neufchatel, the brilliant portraitist, precisely in the development of these reportorial qualities he possessed himself. The development of two brilliant painters from the same atelier argues that Coeck had some merit as a teacher. The parallel tendencies of Bruegel and Neufchatel (or Lucidel) would seem to offer additional proof of this. Bruegel became the painter of the people, their ideas, customs and traditions; Neufchatel developed into a profound and sober portraitist. In connection with the last, Alphonse Wauters observed, to be quoted by van Bastelaer who is again saluted by the present author, that "it was principally through the art of portraiture that the national genius protested against the invasion of Italianism during the entire period between the death of Metsys and the coming of Rubens."

A further evidence of the influence of Coeck may be deduced from the fact that if Bruegel was so great a master of painting in distemper, as is generally conceded, he owed his facility to his master in whose atelier numerous patterns for tapestries were executed. If Bruegel also acquired a facility in pen and ink work, this may also be attributed to Coeck whom some have considered Georgione's equal in this medium.

After having been first the student of Peter Coeck, to return once more to van Mander, Bruegel became the disciple of Jerome Cock.

For some reason or other, the scholars are agreed that Bruegel's first association with Jerome Cock lasted but a short while, and was due only to the fact that Peter Coeck died a few months short of the period Bruegel needed to finish his apprenticeship and qualify as a free-master. Since Bruegel is to work with Cock for several years after returning from Italy and will be profoundly affected by his association with him, we can briefly outline Cock's position at this time.

Jerome Cock had established himself in Antwerp in 1546, opening a shop called the *Sign of the Four Winds*. He was a painter without patrons, but a successful merchant who sold engravings, reproductions of masterpieces, and a variety of subjects that appealed to the popular taste. His fat, mustached wife sat at the cashier's desk, and supervised a trade that made them wealthy enough to build an impressive house a few doors from the town-hall. In the brief period he spent as apprentice to Cock, Bruegel must have done plenty of dirty work for his master, copying, engraving, and likely as not, waiting on trade and framing pictures.

Finally, in 1551, Bruegel was admitted to his guild as a master, a fact with which you must be thoroughly bored by this time because of its frequent mention. The date, at this juncture, signals Bruegel's departure for Italy on the *wanderjahr* which was practically compulsory for every Flemish painter who wanted to get work and make money. Anent this voyage, many critics have wondered why "peasant" Bruegel would have wanted to go to Italy when there was nothing to interest him or profit his art among the elegances of an over-civilized people. This is taking a good deal for granted. Bruegel, at the time of his journey to Rome, is still a young painter with probably a good deal more cleverness than greatness. It probably can be said that far from

33

having developed the highly personalized point of view of the period of 1559-1569, he was as thoroughly Italianized as any of his contemporaries and it was only later, when his genius manifested itself, that he rebelled against the imitation of another culture.

Of his journey to Rome we know nothing except that he went by way of France. No work of Bruegel's, dating from the year 1552, has come down to us and the scholars have often wondered whether so great a genius as Bruegel could have let a year out of his life go by without making marks on paper. In connection with this point Paul Colin (*Bruegel le Vieux*) offers the suggestion that Bruegel made the journey on foot. This sounds extremely likely. Where would a young master who had just left his apprenticeship get enough money to do the trip in style? If he did tramp his way, and this was a far more popular method of getting places in the 16th Century than it is now, he could hardly have carried brush, colors, and canvas with him.

In 1553, we know, Bruegel reached Rome. He did two landscapes in this year, both of which still exist. They are purely academic in feeling and of no other interest than that they mark the first appearance of the genre in the artist's catalogue. Van Bastelaer puts a good deal more importance on these two sketches than the works themselves can easily bear. He declares that Bruegel develops an appetite for grandiose perspectives, a matter of reasoning strictly after the fact. For although Bruegel, in crossing the Alps to return home, does an enormous number of landscapes, the two completed in Rome can hardly be considered an indication of what is to come.

Further material on the Italian sojourn is largely conjecture.

"Before returning across the Alps," says van Bastelaer, for example, "he spent some time in Sicily." This statement is offered on the basis of Bruegel's famous *Combat Naval* depicting a battle between enemy fleets in the Straight of Messina. This work was to be engraved by Francois Huys in 1561 for Jerome Cock, Bruegel's publisher.

Paul Colin, whose disagreements with other critics form as large a part of his text as do those of the present author, takes sharp issue with van Bastelaer on this point. He observes that there is no certitude of a Sicilian visit whatever, that if *Combat Naval* represents the Straight of Messina, perhaps Bruegel was inspired by an Italian engraving. Further, asseverates Colin, the trip to Naples was not usual, in 1552, unless Brueghel had gone there to embark for home by way of Marseilles. Since the painter returned to the Netherlands by way of the Brenner Pass, this possibility is eliminated. Colin suggests that Bruegel's *Combat Naval* might also have owed its origin to an anecdote of the widely travelled Peter Coeck, Bruegel's first master who had seen, among other things, the siege of Tunis. But in any case, Colin refuses to allow that a little known and inhospitable country would have been visited by a young artist who was not only poor but had little time to waste.

The picture itself, *Combat Naval* is an extraordinary work and well worth a word or two. The boldness of the drawing, the fact that the artist never tries to modify his viewpoint to secure a familiar aspect, admitting the most accidental effects that perspective presents, has been observed by several analysts of Bruegel's art. One aesthetician sees, in this marine, Bruegel sharing Bosch's love of rarety, in his many-sided study of the

35

boats, and the *beginning of the modern hatred for the already-seen.* The author of this note lives on a somewhat less intellectual level than the last of the foregoing critics, and an aspect of *Combat Naval* that charms him is that these boats and dolphins of Bruegel supplied models for all the map makers beginning with the *Evitas Orbis Terrarum.* The little caravels you see on both old maps and those in Mr. Van Loon's *Geography,* were inspired by this work of Bruegel's which has otherwise such an impressive message.

Before passing to the landscapes done by Bruegel on his way back to Antwerp, the first important manifestation of his art, it might be well to consider the wonderment of a certain critic that no figure studies appear to have been done by him in Rome. With the exception of the minute characters that animate *Saint Jerome in the Desert,* there is no study or sketch that has come down to us, nor does any reminiscence of Italy in the way of costume or other peculiarity appear in his later work. That this should seem strange, when one considers the material that we have from this period consists of two landscapes, seems doubly strange to the present author. The fact that both landscapes were done in pen and ink can also be considered something less than remarkable. Perhaps Bruegel couldn't afford panels, canvas, or colors. Bruegel's entire Roman trip can be considered, to repeat a notion expressed before, the typical journey of a Flemish painter of the Italian period, seeking of the masters the tricks of their style. If one doesn't view the artist's early life in the light of his later genius, one will not be tempted to credit him for prodigies intellect of which he was still incapable.

The portion of the Alps painted by Bruegel on his way home

is generally thought to be the Tyrol. Judging by the number of studies he did, the mountain scenery had a profoundly moving effect on him. From what we can deduce of his itinerary, on first leaving Antwerp, we can readily understand this. Leaving Flanders, in the flat north country, journeying through the more travelled highways of France on foot, entering Italy by way of the Corniche Road, Bruegel had never, probably, seen anything of the majestic uplands. In Italy, the Appenines are little more than hills. But on his way home, when he first glimpsed the towering snow-topped heights of the Alps, he felt the stir of an inspiration which was his first spur to greatness. Walking through the Brenner, beside the deep, swiftly flowing river with its dull surface reflecting only the rocky cliffs that tower above its banks, seeing the occasional, unbelievably green meadows, lush with the heavy dews and frequent rains, overwhelmed by distant views of the peaks that crowd the horizon, the depth of his emotions is evident from his landscapes. He appears to have stayed in the neighborhood of Innsbruck and done studies so numerous that van Mander was to report: "he swallowed the mountains and rocks of the Alps to vomit them, when he returned, upon panels and canvas." It is interesting to note, in connection with his sketches, that deeply moved as he was by what he saw, Bruegel's representations were sufficiently realistic and respectful of nature for certain of the scenes to be exactly located.

With this first participation of his own powerful individuality in an art which hitherto consisted of principles crammed as though for an examination, Bruegel's development really began. A conflict between his instinct for reality and his academic train-

37

ing is apparent from this point until 1563, when he finally freed himself of all uncertainties. What Colin has called "the tourmented silhouette of the Alps" entruded into his lowland sketches and absurd geographical contradictions frequently appeared in his work, a melange of Italian reminiscences and verities of the soil. It was this last which was to preserve his identity for him upon his return to Antwerp.

Bruegel was back in the Netherlands at the end of 1553. He resumed his place at Jerome Cock's, not as a student this time, but as what might be called a staff artist. He had to earn his living somehow, and although Antwerp was one of the richest towns in Europe and its wealthy burghers could afford to cultivate a taste for the arts, an "unknown" had just as hard a time as he has now. Bruegel, about 27 or 28 years old, had to get a job and it can be said that he didn't do badly in picking the shrewd, highly intelligent Jerome Cock for an employer. Until Bruegel's removal to Brussels, when he married in 1563, he furnished Cock's engravers with a steady stream of drawings and doubtless drew the large part of his income from this source. It was Cock, too, who had him do pieces for the popular taste in the manner of Jerome Bosch, and in coming under the influence of this last artist, he was to give his own work its finally definitive direction. There was to come a time, it is true, when Cock's influence became a hindering one. Bruegel was to face the choice between a definite income from giving the public what it wanted in terms of Cock's canny estimation of the popular taste, or following his own serious bent towards a profound and highly personal art.

At present, however . . . the time is 1554 . . . Bruegel is at least five years away from this crisis, and he contents himself with turning out work that will win his bread. The first things he did for Cock were a series of Alpine and Italian landscapes, indicating not only his own preoccupations but those of his employer who personally favored the genre. Shortly afterward, an engraving: *Pasturage Before the St. George Gate* was executed from his drawing, a foreshadowing of his later realism. But more important than this, as an indicator, is *Le Patinage* (Skating), a first manifestation of his interest in rustic subjects, and a sign, one feels, of the joy he must have experienced at returning to his own country after a two year exile. You can imagine the delight of this young peasant at seeing once again the familiar frosty scenes that would have seemed hale and invigorating after the warm Roman winters. Technically, this picture contains the same conception of the accessory role of figures in a landscape which characterizes his first paintings of the 1559 period. There can also be seen in *Le Patinage,* the sobriety of line necessary where figures are subordinate to landscape, the restriction only to such detail as makes character, the great realistic style which the artist will preserve all throughout the period in which the importance of the figure increases until it finally dominates. There is one other major implication in *Le Patinage,* one which should logically have come first, perhaps, but which we have held back until this point for purposes of transition: the influence of Jerome Bosch.

It is largely through Bosch that Bruegel became aware of the nature of his own genius. When Flemish painting turned towards Italy half a century before, Jerome Bosch obstinately resisted this tendency and tapped the resources of medieval folk poetry for his diableries and illustrations of folklore. Fanciful and imaginative as was his subject matter, it was depicted in terms of the most unrelenting realism. For the monsters he drew, Bosch sought human models with the fervor of an anthropologist. In his reaction against the idealism of his contemporaries and the smooth repetitious works of the court painters like Memling and David, no aberration from their conventionalized concept of the human form was too enormous for him to seize and transfer to canvas. His moralities found an immediate and popular audience in the rude and somewhat scatalogical Flemish temperament, and it was this audience, in imitating Bosch, that Bruegel was to find still eager for these appeals to its own taste, fifty years later.

Bruegel modified Bosch's realism. He did not seek to particularize on the difference between human countenances to the degree that the faces in a picture had all to be stamped with some abnormality. He was not interested in painting the malformed for its own sake. Even in his own diabolisms, he took less exceptional forms for his models, was more interested in the moral implication of his subject than the physical misery of his figures. In this sense, he elevated his art, in its respect for character, to one of real social significance.

Before going on to discuss the period of Bosch's influence . . . we have a section dedicated to this phase a little further on . . . we feel it necessary to indicate that there is a tendency to overinterpret it. For after Bruegel had done a certain amount of work in this vein, he absorbed all the impetus it could provide him with. His further development was strictly in terms of his own individuality. Yet there is a considerable feeling among the critics that certain inferior canvases of Bruegel's best period, *lle Griet,* are influenced wholly by Bosch whose effect

40

the painter should long since have left behind. It should be seen, however, that Bruegel, in painting a work like the *Dulle Griet* at the period when he did, was probably executing a commission for a client. It must be remembered that the popular taste of the period favored these allegories and fantasies and that Bruegel, after using folk lore as the bridge into realism, still had to earn his living by giving his patrons, at least occasionally, what they wanted.

With Bruegel's encountering the influence of Bosch, his art has developed to the point where we can divide it into several categories, examine each, and put an end to this inquiry.

The first of these is the folk-lore period, with its tales, proverbs, customs and superstitions. They provide him with the opportunity to depict the faces, manners and gestures of the common people of his time.

The second period begins in 1563 with the artist's marriage and removal to Brussels, where, exiled from his easy-living friends and the effortless livelihood that his association with Cock gave him, he was delivered, as certain critics will have it, to his own inspiration. This period is characterized by the particular seriousness of his subject matter, an indication, too, of the troubled times and bloody repressions of which a Marxist criticism soon to appear, will make much. It is at this point that Bruegel produces his group of what will have to be called religious pictures, for want of a better name. All are animated by a more or less dramatic realism, and several symbolize the artist's reactions to the troubles through which his country was struggling.

The final phase is that in which Bruegel, at last in complete

41

possession of the liberty that was destined to be his, simplifies his compositions, reducing his figures to a few, abandoning all pretence of literary, historical or didactic purpose to create purely realistic subjects. To this period belong the *Wedding Feast, Kermess,* and the great canvases representing the seasons.

*   *   *

Let us begin, then, with the period of Bosch's influence, one on which you were promised a few remarks some pages back. Unlike Bosch, Bruegel was not interested in witchcraft or sorcery in the sense that absorption in evil is another phase of religiosity, the obverse of good, the shadowy half of the entity into which theology divided the universe. Neither the engravings nor the paintings were in Bosch's vein of demonology but were allegories from contemporary folklore. In spite of their debt to Bosch, the works of this period contain more fantasy and wit than sincere mysticism. It was impossible for Bruegel's genius, a certain critic feels, and this is in face of a considerable movement to make a conscious humanist of Old Peter, to subscribe to this state of mind with any sincerity. Since the genre was in fashion, he did many subjects in its tradition but always with complete objectivity. He borrowed from Bosch the traditional characters and fashioned them into representations that were not dogmatic but symbolic, at the same time filling them with a spirit that was earthly and realistic. It was this lesson of realism that he abstracted from Bosch, a matter we have pointed out so often that it is bound to have made itself plain.

Among the paintings of the first period, the *Combat of Carni-*

42

val and Lent deserves attention, not only for its content but because it is one of Bruegel's first canvases. His previous work had been done, as you've doubtless gathered, in other media. Some attention must be given here, whether you dislike the digression or not, to the phenomenon of Bruegel's first canvas appearing at such a late time. Some scholar will probably observe that Bruegel was, after all, only about 30 years old, but still this painting is belated when one considers that his career was to terminate with his death only ten years afterward. The question has been asked: had he not painted before this period? It must be concluded, in view of the technical qualities of his first dated oil, that he must certainly have had considerable experience with the medium. Further, the material he had given the engravers prior to this date was not sufficient to have absorbed all his time. It is generally thought that the practice of painting in distemper, popular in those times, resulted in the disappearance of much of his work. It is known that nothing whatever remains of the product of certain painters who devoted themselves solely to this impermanent medium.

To return, then, to *Carnaval and Lent,* an analysis shows Bruegel a long way from the peak he was subsequently to reach. An indiscriminate juxtaposition of countless episodes without any connection or interdependence evidences a startling compositional weakness. The central anecdote does not even require the attention of the closest onlookers whereas it might have been the psychological nucleus of the composition. It should be observed, on the other hand, that certain detail, like the fishwives by the well, shows Bruegel no longer inventing, but observing minutely the character of his own people, the face of his own country. Un-

43

like the typical humanist that critics like Karoly Tolnai try to make him, he was not to seek a pretentious wisdom from a culture dead for centuries. He was to find about him an inspiration that sprang from his own peasant breeding, one which he was to cling to with good peasant sense.

Children's Games, another painting of this period, shows Bruegel still facing the same compositional difficulties, still rendering a curious, illogical and encyclopedic view of his subject. But in this picture will also be found a far more direct expression of his own emotions than *Carnaval and Lent,* a vivid life that can engage one's attention for hours. Fascinated, one discovers the same games that are played today. Children roll hoops, whip tops, play leap-frog and a rough game called *Johnny Ride the Pony* at which the author broke an ankle many years ago. Of course, this quality in *Children's Games* is identical with that in *Paddington Station* at which Clive Bell, Roger Fry and the author of *Apples and Madonnas* look down their noses. Nevertheless, Bruegel and this canvas have a different relation to the history of art than the contriver of *Paddington Station,* used so often by the moderns as a stalking horse.

All the work of this first or folklore period is stamped with a singular gaiety. The proverbs and allegories are not particularly pessimistic and the other small subjects are all linked in one way or another with the fetes and diversions of the times. The scholars seem to be agreed that much of Bruegel's attitude, during this time, can be traced to the influence exercised by his friend Hans Franckert, his continual companion.

Hans Franckert was a merchant . . . of what, no one seems to know . . . who moved to Antwerp from Nuremberg in 1546. Van

PIETER BRUEGHEL

17. DETAIL FROM WINTER—THE FIRE

18. DETAIL FROM CARNIVAL AND FAST (CHURCH)

19. STORMY SEA

20. BATTLE OF MT. GILBOA

21. THE ROAD TO CALVARY

22. DETAIL FROM THE PEASANT WEDDING

23. DETAIL FROM THE CHILDREN'S GAME

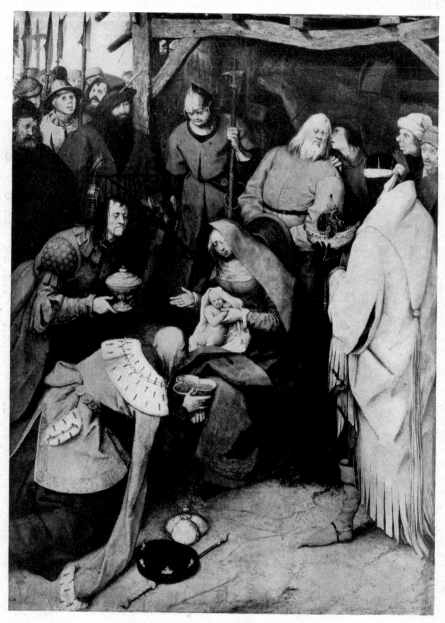

24. THE ADORATION OF THE MAGI

Bastelaer credits him with calling Bruegel's attention to rustic subject matter which he had gotten to know through the German engravers. This critic also declares that Franckert ordered many paintings from his friend, a matter which would be very important if it could be proved. Paul Colin, on the other hand, sees in Franckert the sole merit of having introduced Bruegel to the banker Jonghelinck who commissioned the series of paintings known as *The Seasons.* Karoly Tolnai and the Platonists see Franckert as a member of one of the humanist groups of Antwerp and the sponsor of what they would have one believe is the philosophic content of Bruegel's art.

As far as any facts exist on the relationship between Bruegel and Franckert, van Mander is once again the sole source. He declares, simply, that Bruegel enjoyed going to the kermesses and village feasts with Franckert, both disguised as peasants. They mingled with the crowd and even claimed relationiship with one or another of the families at rustic weddings, bringing gifts to assure themselves of a welcome.

That this slender information has been interpreted in so many different ways, is characteristic of writers seeking occasions to display their own powers at the expense of their subject matter. Colin visualizes Bruegel living precariously from day to day without any regard for bourgeois conformism, running wild with a shopkeeper whose idea of a good time was to play house with the trollops of the countryside. Van Bastelaer, more seriously, cautions the reader lest he think Bruegel was a high liver, always ready to carouse and drink. If Bruegel frequented the feasts, carnivals, and folk celebrations of his time, observes this critic, he was always the artist in search of material; his work indicates he must have sketched while the others enjoyed themselves.

It should be enough, one feels, to know from van Mander that Bruegel's interest in country manners was inspired directly by life.

Van Mander's description of Bruegel, gathered from contemporaries who had known the painter, enables us for the first time to get some idea of what he looked like. He appears to have been a quiet steady man who, like all great observers, spoke little. His fine distinguished face had a determined cast, eyes large and penetrating. His mouth, framed by a heavy mustache and slightly curly beard, was both sensitive and faintly scoffing. Van Mander adds that Bruegel, though taciturn, was a good fellow in company and took particular delight in telling ghost stories and horror tales to his students.

In 1563, towards the end of the first stage in his development outlined before, the comparatively good times turned Bruegel's thoughts towards marriage. The disastrous wars that had torn Europe seemed over with the marriage of Philip II and Mary Tudor, and the Treaty of Cateau Cambresis. The land was the happiest and richest in Europe and a man might well think of founding a family. The artist was 33, enjoyed the patronage of Cardinal Granvelle, and was admired for the great landscape engravings and the two paintings previously discussed. Before he could marry, and there is reason to believe that he had picked out the girl of his choice some time before he was free to propose to her, Bruegel had to get rid of a mistress with whom he had been living for quite a while. It appears that she was an incorrigible liar and the artist, telling her that she must remedy this if she would have him marry her, cut a notch in a stick for

46

every falsehood she told. The strategem worked, for the girl was unable to stop lying and Bruegel had soon whittled his measuring rod into a splinter.

Rid of this incubus, Bruegel sought for his wife, Marie Coeck, the daughter of his first master, the same whom he had carried in his arms as an infant. Marie was the child of Coeck's second wife, Verhulst Bessemers, a rather unusual woman who was a miniaturist of account, according to Guichardin. When Coeck had died, 13 years before, she had moved to Brussels; it was she, apparently, who insisted that if Bruegel marry Marie, he must move to Brussels where he would not be tempted by his dissolute companions and his former mistress. So in 1563, at Easter time, Bruegel celebrated his marriage at the Church of the Chapel and settled down to a new life which was to terminate prematurely some six and a half years later.

Most critics attribute the rapid growth of Bruegel's art from this point onwards, to his marriage. His exile from Antwerp is considered another primary factor. Deprived of his expeditions with Franckert to the fetes, he is declared to have been delivered wholly to his own inspirations and enabled to bring to his work a power which the gayer subjects of his celibate days could not call forth. Thus the new material, more adequate to his natural sobriety of line, is accounted for.

The present author notes these rather impressionistic theories for what they're worth, but sees fit to point out that the political complexion of the times, which had abruptly changed, may well have been responsible for Bruegel's new direction. On this point, a Marxist analysis soon to be published will provide comment. Meanwhile, however, we can indicate briefly that the accession of Philip II, the continual presence of Spanish troops on Flemish soil, the burdensome taxes and levies were rapidly providing the basis for the War of Liberation.

Of the paintings of this period, the *Road to Calvary*, 1564, has been commented upon by Mr. Huxley. Since this *Note on Peter Bruegel* is sharing a book with Mr. Huxley's essay, the author will avoid repetition where possible. It can be said of the *Calvary*, however, that its reality is such that the scene might have been one that Bruegel witnessed at Antwerp or Brussels.

The *Adoration of the Magi*, 1564, can be dismissed as a scene in the Italian manner played by Flemish actors; it is on a level still remote from the painter's best work. The next canvas, however, *The Massacre of the Innocents*, is a subject finally worthy of the artist's mettle. It shows him ready to abandon the vast ensembles with tiny figures and attempt simple dramatic groups with more important principals. We have no wish to overinterpret this painting but we do feel that it was directly inspired by the country's bitter troubles and that the artist's anguished awareness was responsible for the new simplification and power evident in this work. The period, as pointed out, is one of bloody repressions, penal edicts against heretics, dread of the Spanish Inquisition. An insurrection of the lower classes with the destruction of one of the greatest of medieval cathedrals is to follow close on the heels of 1564. The Duke of Alva and his "Council of Blood" are to provoke a widespread rebellion that will become an almost hundred years war. *The Massacre of the Innocents*, with its motionless, rigidly disciplined battalion of lancers stationed center in brutal contrast to the frightful episodes which are taking place on all sides of it, is a symbol of oppression so elo-

48

quent that no further explanation of it is necessary. The fact that the artist lived in Brussels, where the "troubles" had only a political aspect and presented no such spectacles to the man on the street is evidence of a powerful imagination and a newly found ability to project it.

The final invasion of religious by realistic subject matter has taken place, and the period of Bruegel's greatest work is at hand. The figures take a more important place in his compositions; the style of their contours is refined without changing their former spirit. The artist, at a time when the Italian mannerism is more pronounced than ever, in the Low Countries, becomes not only the first realist in modern art, but the greatest one.

Before detailing whatever observations we have to offer on this final period in Bruegel's development, we have a last opportunity to comment on the artist personally from the small stock of anecdotage that has come down to us. The painter's work, feels one critic (inevitably a Frenchman) reflects the preoccupation of a well-balanced, and hence married, life. Bruegel, "about to be blessed with a son," as this man puts it, devotes himself soberly to his art like a *bon bourgeois* full of the responsibilities of approaching parenthood. We have already made comment, by implication, on this attribution of a typically suburban character to Peter Bruegel. We are not inclined to rate paternity as a force to bring out greatness in an artist. However, in spite of the coming parturition (which might not, after all, have been novel in his experience) Bruegel kept his sense of humor. An anecdote recounted by van Mander, one which seems, moreover, to have escaped retelling as far as we can discover, shows that Bruegel could still manage to laugh and from the belly at that.

49

It seems that Jean Vredeman de Vriese, who was the creator of the Flemish Renaissance style along with Cornelius Floris, had been commissioned to do a mural for Arnold Molckeman, military paymaster and counsellor of Brussels. The painting was in an illusory perspective which Vredeman particularly fancied: a summer house in the middle of an elaborately geometrical garden. One day, Bruegel dropped in to look at his colleague's work while Vredeman was at lunch. Finding himself before the unfinished painting with palette, brushes and colors ready to hand, Bruegel couldn't resist the temptation to add a touch of his own to the relentlessly formal design. In a door opening in the wall of Vredeman's carefully drawn garden, Bruegel painted a peasant in baggy pants and dirty smock, very very much in the good graces of a peasant woman. When it was discovered, the joke was so widely appreciated that under no circumstances would Molckeman allow Vredeman to efface this comment on his work.

We have already generalized so much about the rustic subjects of Bruegel's last period that only a few observations remain to be made. In *The Peasant Dance* (Kermess) and *The Wedding Feast,* he has abandoned the elevated viewpoint from which he painted the famous landscapes and adopted a low perspective which emphasizes the new importance of the figure. Both canvases represent the goal of Bruegel's development: underived and uninfluenced realism. They observe with pitiless detail, the customs, gestures, and faces of the peasants. These faces, of which there are so many in Bruegel's figure paintings, demonstrate once more a sympathy and an understanding that none of Bruegel's followers or imitators was to possess. Frozen into grimaces by the cold, seared with squint lines by the summer sun, they make painful contrast with the festive backgrounds against which they find themselves. The peasants love a good time and on the rare occasions when they are freed from the fields and the manure piles, they get drunk, gorge themselves with food, force their work-shackled muscles to caper in unaccustomed dances. But their faces never lose the dull, brutal cast that their work has set upon them.

Besides these two oils, which are illustrated in color in this book, Bruegel did a series of pieces whose ironic symbolism definitely argues a political consciousness. The *Pays de Cocagne* (The Land of Cockaigne) is an imaginative illustration of the folk legend of the lazy glutton. Cakes hang from trees like leaves, newly laid eggs walk up to one's plate, freshly plucked and roasted chickens lay their heads on the platter waiting for the sated gourmands to dispose of them. All this plenty is in mock contrast to the Netherlands under the regency of Margaret of Parma, and one is certain that the public for which Bruegel's work was intended understood and relished the irony as well as anyone might with an empty stomach and cornucopiae all around him.

The Parable of the Blind has the same contemporary inspiration as the *Land of Cockaigne, The Good and Bad Shepherd, The Shepherd fleeing the Wolf, The Proverb of the Bird Nester, The Beggars* (Les Mendiants . . . Louvre), and *The Magpie on the Gibbet.* These are, apparently, the last canvases Bruegel painted. It seems incredible that commentators like Paul Colin can deny the obviously symbolic nature of these pieces, several of which could even be called propagandist.

The first of the group, *Parable of the Blind,* is considered one of the masterpieces of all painting. The artist's fixed compositional pattern: a strong diagonal dividing the panel into foreground for figures, background for landscape, recurs. In this instance, however, the low perspective that emphasizes the figures avoids the monotony that one inevitably feels before the landscapes. The title, the blind leading the blind, relates sufficiently to the political troubles of the times to require little further explanation. Specifically, however, the artist's ironic fancy has made the leaders even more sightless, if that's possible, than those they guide. Great hollow sockets mar their faces while those behind them seem to receive, at least, sensations of light, holding their faces up in that straining, open-mouthed fashion that we all know.

It was in connection with this canvas that Paul Colin observed that Bruegel did not paint with any political or philosophic considerations in mind but was concerned solely with his aesthetic.

This was the year, 1568, that the Duke of Alva came with 20,000 Spanish soldiers by way of Genoa, Savoy and the *Franche Comté* to the Netherlands, to begin his regency. Margaret of Parma and her advisor, Granvelle, resigned. The last, the present author feels certain, is symbolized in the *Shepherd Fleeing the Wolf*. Thousands of Netherlanders left the country, the Counts of Egmont and Hoorn were executed, the estates of those who did not appear before Alva's *Council of Blood* were confiscated (among them those of William of Orange). An arbitrary tax consisting of one tenth the price of every income was imposed! Do these sound like times when a painter, or anyone else who possessed some means of calling attention to injustice or expressing his own hatred of oppression, could devote himself to the purely formal aspects of his art? The analogy with modern times is inescapable. Those who cannot see the revolutionary in the paintings of this period prefer like Paul Colin, the inevitable betrayal of too rigid a point-of-view, or the affliction that is the subject of *Parable of the Blind.*

In the *Beggars* (Les Mendiants), a small panel that hangs in the Louvre, Colin sees the artist fashioning a beautiful, luminous corner of nature, indifferent to the miseries of man. This refers, apparently, to the almost microscopic scene visible in the background of a painting whose principal focus lies in the center of a group of cripples. These last, moreover, wear the fox-tail symbol of the beggar's party, opponents of Spain. (Hence the title). Did Bruegel dream of a political interpretation, asks Colin? Must one see a satire against the Duke of Alva's government? It is possible, he admits, but he feels it more likely that the master was simply diverted by the contrast presented by the misery of the humans depicted, against the delicate light of a summer morning. This interpretation appears as absurd to the present author as do the vapourings of Karoly Tolnai and the platonists to Mr. Colin.

Bruegel's last canvas, *The Magpie on the Gibbet,* was a dying gift to his wife, according to van Mander. It was the only one left of a group of paintings Bruegel ordered destroyed during his last illness. It is conjectured that these works were so symbolically critical of Alva's régime that the painter feared they would bring trouble to his wife and infant sons. The meaning of *Magpie on the Gibbet* is obvious. The peasants dance in the shadow of the gallows, either from indifference, or desperation, or that strange humor that seems to increase with the unfitness of its occasion . . . like the temptation to burst out laughing at a funeral, or interrupt a sermon with a flatulent raspberry. The figures again occupy the left foreground into which the diagonal divides the panel. The background is an extraordinarily charming landscape wherein a winding river finds its way through a summer countryside. The trick of the viewpoint gives the observer that curiously elevated feeling, makes the picture a dramatic one that not only carries the eye down into the landscape but the beholder himself.

The painter could not have chosen to leave a more fitting last work than *Magpie on the Gibbet*. It combines all the best aspects of Bruegel's art while remaining an indivisible and organic whole.

By way of last remarks, we would like to say a few words about the large panel called *Summer* although Mr. Huxley has already commented on the series of which it forms part. The painting hangs in the Metropolitan Museum of Art and is one that most of the readers of this book will be able to see. Compositionally, the painting is weak with an excessive detail that contributes little to the abstract subject: the season of plenty. It has been observed by one lyrical commentator that this painting indicates the artist preferred drama to the elegy, the hymn to romance. Bruegel, in short, was more at home with the sober and eloquent backgrounds of winter than with the lush imaginary summer that certainly never existed in Flanders while the present author was there. But in this one, and let us say inferior work, there may be seen that quality in Bruegel which particularly wins the sympathies today of all art-lovers who know themselves to be members of the same class which Bruegel painted. At the foot of the tree, in the right foreground, lies a man. When you have absorbed the general effect that the composition and color have had upon you and draw nearer to examine the painting in detail, this recumbent figure looms larger and larger until it represents an instinct in the painter which still awaits analysis by a competent critic. The harvester, the man who works with his hands, the antithesis of everything that interested Bruegel's elegant contemporaries, in short: the proletarian, lies there in the center of this huge panel, savagely possessed by the kind of sleep that only the working class knows. His brown slit of a mouth is half open, his thick legs are outspread in utter exhaustion. When you have seen this figure and then wandered through the galleries of the Museum and looked at the art of other schools and other epochs, so remote, it seems, from the forces that affect your life, Breugel's might as a painter will be revealed to you even though he be represented here by one of his lesser works.

The price of $1.25 per volume, set for this series, is far below the usual cost of such books. The WILLEY BOOK CO. will make every effort to maintain this low price in order that everyone may collect the entire series and so build a fine art library and picture gallery.

EL GRECO (*Domenicos Theotocopulos*) *by* P. HANDELMAN

El Greco's canvasses are characterized by a modern feeling due in part to the rigorous restraint of his palette and his dramatic anatomical distortions.

The text surveys the position of El Greco with particular emphasis on his role of teacher, thru the example of his living canvasses, to Cézanne, Monet and whole schools of Impressionists and Moderns.

Among the plates included in this book, many are reproduced in color for the first time.

THOMAS ROWLANDSON *by* ART YOUNG

Some artists are revered because of the enviable places they occupy in the history of art and others admired for their technical dexterity and craftsmanship. Rowlandson stands apart from any of these as an artist who is loved because of the viewpoint he represents and the vigorous honesty of his painting.

Art Young is a worker in the same fields of art that Rowlandson labored in and writes about his subject with a sympathetic understanding such as only an artist can give to another.

MEXICAN ARTISTS AND MURALS

Diego Rivera, José Orozco and the other practicing mural painters of Mexico, many of them anonymous, pride themselves on being workmen, content to receive workmen's wages in return for paintings dedicated to the people.

ASK YOUR BOOKSELLER ABOUT THESE BOOKS